WATCH THIS SPACE!

The SOLAR SYSTEM, METEORS, and COMETS

CRABTREE
Publishing Company
www.crabtreebooks.com

Crabtree Publishing Company
www.crabtreebooks.com
1-800-387-7650

Published in Canada
Crabtree Publishing
616 Welland Avenue
St. Catharines, ON
L2M 5V6

Published in the United States
Crabtree Publishing
PMB 59051
350 Fifth Ave, 59th Floor
New York, NY 10118

Author: Clive Gifford
Editorial director: Kathy Middleton
Editors: Izzi Howell, Shirley Duke
Designer: Clare Nicholas
Cover design and concept: Lisa Peacock
Proofreaders: Kathy Middleton
Prepress technician: Ken Wright
Print and production coordinator: Margaret Amy Salter

Published by Crabtree Publishing Company in 2016

First published in 2015 by Wayland
Copyright © Wayland, 2015

The website addresses (URLs) included in this book were valid at the time of going to press. However, it is possible that contents or addresses may have changed since the publication of this book. No responsibility for any such changes can be accepted by either the author or the Publisher.

Printed in the USA/082015/SN20150529

Picture credits:
Shutterstock/A-R-T cover (background), Shutterstock/Vadim Sadovski cover (tl), Dreamstime/Maxcortesiphoto cover (tc), Shutterstock/Tristan3D cover (bl), Shutterstock/Petrafler cover (bc), Shutterstock/Antony McAulay cover (br), Shutterstock/A-R-T title page (background), NASA/JPL title page (tl), Shutterstock/David Woods, Shutterstock/3drenderings, NASA, NASA/JPL, NASA Planetary Photojournal title page (b l-r), Shutterstock/Festa 4(bl), Shutterstock/Kapreski (br), William Donohoe/Rocket Design 4–5, Science Photo Library/Gary Hincks 6 (tl), Thinkstock/Dawn Hudson 6 (bl), Dreamstime/Snapgalleria 7 (cl), NASA 7 (tr), NASA/JPL/University of Arizona 7 (br), Shutterstock/oorka 8 (bl), NASA 8–9 (tc), Dreamstime/Julynx 9 (cr), Science Photo Library/Mark Garlick 9 (br), Shutterstock/David Woods 10, NASA 11 (tl), Thinkstock/7immy 11 (bl), Shutterstock/Happy Art 11 (bc), Shutterstock/David Carillet 11 (r), NASA/Johns Hopkins University Applied Physics Laboratory/Carnegie Institution of Washington 12 (tl), NASA 12 (cl), Shutterstock/stockakia 12 (b), Shutterstock/RedKoala 13 (bl), NASA/JPL 13 (tr and cr), NASA/JPL 14 (tl), NASA/MOLA Science Team/O. de Goursac, Adrian Lark 14 (bl), Shutterstock/gbreezy 15 (bl), NASA/JPL-Caltech/MSSS 15 (tr), Shutterstock/RedKoala 15 (br), NASA/JPL-Caltech/Eyes 16 , Shutterstock/Danil Balashov and Shutterstock/Zaytseva Darya 17 (bl), Shutterstock/MarcelClemens 17 (tr), Shutterstock/RedKoala 17 (br), Shutterstock/ MarcelClemens 18, Shutterstock/jehsomwang and Shutterstock/ Jef Thompson 19 (tl), Shutterstock/uranus 19 (tr), NASA/NSSDC Photo Gallery 19 (bc), Shutterstock/3drenderings 20 (l), Shutterstock/ bioraven 20 (r), NASA Planetary Photojournal 21 (tr), NASA/JPL 21 (cr), Dreamstime/Sergey89rus 21 (br), Dreamstime/Johannes Gerhardus Swanepoel 22 (tc), Shutterstock/ Vadim Ermak 22 (bl), Shutterstock/Gl0ck 22 (br), NASA 23 (tr and br), Shutterstock/sripfoto 24–25 (c), Shutterstock/Action Sports Photography 25 (tr), Shutterstock/Happy Art 25 (cr), Shutterstock/lineartestpilot and Shutterstock/dedMazay 25 (br), Shutterstock/Valerio Pardi 26 (l). Shutterstock/timurockart 26 (r), Shutterstock/jorisvo 27 (tr), Shutterstock/ bioraven 27 (cr), J. Linder/ESO 27 (bc), NASA/JPL-Caltech 28, NASA's Goddard Space Flight Center/S. Wiessinger 29 (tl), Shutterstock/uranus 29 (bc), Shutterstock/ILeysen 29 (br)

Design elements throughout: Shutterstock/PinkPueblo, Shutterstock/topform, Shutterstock/Nikiteev_Konstantin, Shutterstock/nienora, Shutterstock/notkoo, Shutterstock/Elinalee, Shutterstock/mhatzapa, Shutterstock/Hilch, Shutterstock/antoninaart

Library and Archives Canada Cataloguing in Publication

Gifford, Clive, author
   The solar system, meteors, and comets / Clive Gifford.

(Watch this space!)
Includes index.
Issued in print and electronic formats.
ISBN 978-0-7787-2027-0 (pbk.).--ISBN 978-0-7787-2023-2 (bound).--
ISBN 978-1-4271-1690-1 (pdf).--ISBN 978-1-4271-1686-4 (html)

   1. Solar system--Juvenile literature. 2. Comets--Juvenile literature. 3. Meteors--Juvenile literature. I. Title.

QB501.3.G54 2015   j523.2   C2015-903185-0
                                          C2015-903186-9

Library of Congress Cataloging-in-Publication Data

Gifford, Clive, author.
The Solar System, meteors, and comets / Clive Gifford.
   pages cm -- (Watch this space!)
"First published in 2015 by Wayland"
 Includes index.
 ISBN 978-0-7787-2023-2 (reinforced library binding : alk. paper) --
 ISBN 978-0-7787-2027-0 (pbk. : alk. paper) --
 ISBN 978-1-4271-1690-1 (electronic pdf : alk. paper) --
 ISBN 978-1-4271-1686-4 (electronic html : alk. paper)
1. Planets--Juvenile literature. 2. Solar system--Juvenile literature. I. Title.

QB602.G54 2016
523.2--dc23
                              2015015368

CONTENTS

MEET THE NEIGHBORS

Earth is not alone. It exists in a star system, called the solar system, along with seven other planets, more than 160 moons, and many other smaller bodies. Formed around five thousand million years ago, the solar system is so big that it would take a passenger airliner flying at over 559 mph (900 km/h) 17 years to travel to Earth from the Sun.

Center Of Attention

At the center of the solar system lies a 863,705-mile- (1,390,000 km) wide star—the Sun. Made almost entirely of hydrogen (71%) and helium (27%) gases and dwarfing all of its neighbors, the Sun contains more than 99% of all the **matter** found in the solar system.

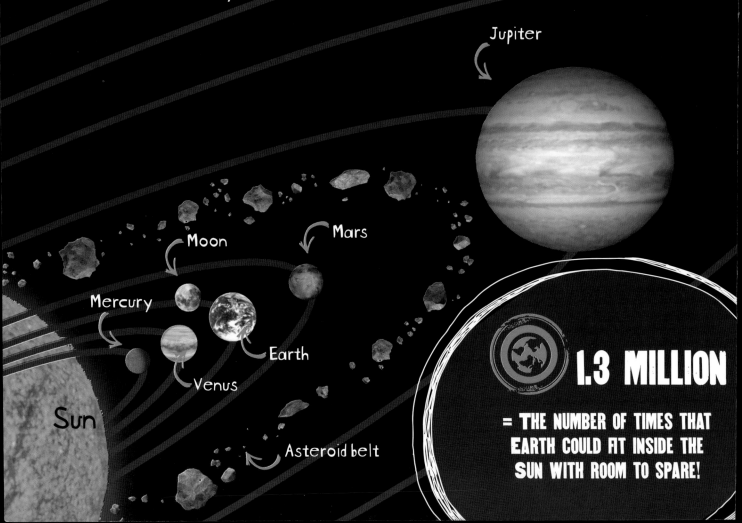

Jupiter

Moon

Mars

Mercury

Earth

Venus

Sun

Asteroid belt

1.3 MILLION

= THE NUMBER OF TIMES THAT EARTH COULD FIT INSIDE THE SUN WITH ROOM TO SPARE!

Inner And Outer

The eight planets that **orbit**, or move around, the Sun are divided into the four inner planets, which are mainly rocky, and the four outer planets, which are much larger and made mostly of gases. Between these two groups lies a broad belt of smaller bodies made of rock and metal called asteroids.

Neptune

Uranus

Saturn

IS NEPTUNE THE END OF THE SOLAR SYSTEM?

Beyond Neptune's orbit, and stretching out as far as 50-55 AU (see box below) from the Sun, lies a cold, mostly empty region of the solar system. Known as the Kuiper Belt, it contains asteroids, Pluto, and a number of other dwarf planets (see page 23).

SOLAR FURNACE

In the Sun's core, a massive nuclear furnace rages with temperatures as high as 59 million°F (15 million°C). The Sun uses up a staggering 661 million tons (600 million metric tons) of hydrogen gas every second, fusing the **nuclei**, or centers, of hydrogen atoms together to form helium atoms. Called a nuclear-fusion reaction, this process generates huge amounts of energy.

ASTRONOMICAL DISTANCES

Because distances in the solar system are so huge, scientists use special units of measurement. An Astronomical Unit (AU) is the average distance between Earth and the Sun—about 93 million miles (150 million km). Mercury is just 0.38 AU from the Sun, while Neptune is a distant 30.1 AU away.

WHAT'S A PLANET, WHAT'S A MOON?

Sun (star)

Earth (planet)

Moon

You may be standing still, but the planet you're on is whizzing through space at 66,611 mph (107,200 km/h). Planets are spherical bodies that travel on a long path around a star. This path is called an orbit. Moons have orbits too, but they move around planets, not stars.

Can You Feel The Force?

Gravity is an invisible yet powerful force of attraction between objects. All objects exert gravity, but the greater an object's mass, which is the amount of matter it contains, the greater its pull of gravity. The Sun's **mass** is so great that it pulls the planets into orbit around it. The time it takes a planet to complete a full orbit of the Sun is called a year.

OVAL ORBITS

A planet's path through space is not a perfect circle. It is more of an ellipse, or oval shape. This means that a planet's distance from the Sun changes throughout its orbit. The point when a planet is farthest from the Sun is known as the aphelion. The point when the planet is nearest to the Sun is called the perihelion.

Spinning Through Space

As planets and moons travel along their orbital paths, each one also moves in another way—spinning on its axis. A complete 360° turn on the **axis** is known as a rotational period or day. Earth's day is 24 hours long. Saturn's day is under 11 hours long. Slow-spinning Venus's day lasts 5,832 hours!

Amazing Moons

Not all moons in the solar system are like Earth's Moon. Neptune's largest moon, Triton, has massive, deep canyons and ice volcanoes which blast out clouds of methane and nitrogen gas. One of Jupiter's moons, Europa, is covered in ice. Below Europa scientists think there may be a giant, underground sea.

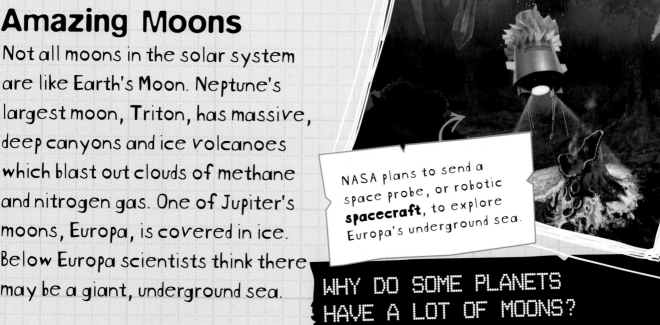

NASA plans to send a space probe, or robotic **spacecraft**, to explore Europa's underground sea.

WHY DO SOME PLANETS HAVE A LOT OF MOONS?

The bigger the planet, the greater its gravity. This means that the gravity of larger planets stretches farther into space and captures more objects. The two biggest planets, Jupiter and Saturn, have more than 60 moons each, while Mercury, the smallest planet, has none.

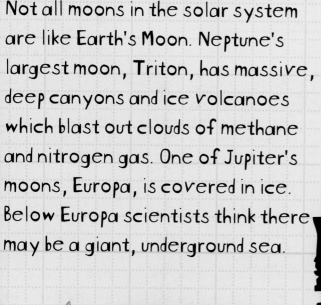

146

= THE NUMBER OF KNOWN MOONS IN THE SOLAR SYSTEM, ACCORDING TO NASA

NO-GO IO

Jupiter's closest moon, Io, is also the solar system's most volcanically active body. Over 400 erupting volcanoes emit clouds of sulfur up to 311 miles (500 km) high and spout out more than 100 times the lava of all the volcanoes on Earth.

The dark spots on Io mark areas of volcanic activity.

PLANET EARTH

Earth was formed around 4.6 billion years ago. It is the only known planet that supports life. Dust, ice, and rock orbiting the newly-formed Sun clumped together and grew in heat and size. The planet cooled, the atmosphere formed, and life on Earth began.

Vital Statistics

Earth is the fifth-largest planet in the solar system and the biggest of the four rocky planets. Its **diameter** at the **equator** is 7,926 miles (12,756 km).

HOW MUCH OF EARTH IS COVERED BY WATER?

About 70% of the Earth's surface is covered by water. About 97% of that is salt water. Most of the fresh water on the planet is locked into the frozen ice caps found at the North and South poles.

mantle

crust

inner core

outer core

EARTH'S COMPOSITION

Earth's inner core is made up of solid iron and nickel, surrounded by an outer core of **molten** iron and nickel. The layer of rock that covers the core is called the mantle and is 1,802 miles (2,900 km) thick. It is mostly solid, but it can bend and twist. The top layer is a thin, brittle crust about 18.6-31 miles (30-50 km) thick on land but only 3-9 miles (5-15 km) on the ocean bed.

IT'S A GAS!

Earth's **atmosphere** is crucial to supporting life because it keeps the planet warm but blocks out harmful **radiation** from space. The atmosphere is composed of 77% nitrogen, 21% oxygen, 1% water vapor, and traces of gases such as argon and carbon dioxide.

At An Angle

Earth is tilted at an angle of 23.5° in relation to the Sun. This tilt creates the seasons on Earth. Summer occurs in the hemisphere, or half of the planet, that is tilted toward the Sun. This allows the Sun's rays to pass through less of Earth's atmosphere and strike part of Earth's surface with greater strength. The hemisphere tilted away from the Sun experiences colder weather.

1.5 MILLION

= THE NUMBER OF DIFFERENT SPECIES OF LIVING THINGS CATALOGED BY SCIENTISTS ON EARTH SO FAR. THE TOTAL NUMBER MAY BE MORE THAN EIGHT MILLION.

Northern hemisphere spring/Southern hemisphere autumn

Northern hemisphere winter/Southern hemisphere summer

Northern hemisphere summer/Southern hemisphere winter

Northern hemisphere autumn/Southern hemisphere spring

THE MOON AND ITS ORBIT

A large object crashed into Earth around 4.5 billion years ago breaking off a chunk which became Earth's Moon. It orbits at an average distance of 238,855 miles (384,400 km) from Earth, which is equal to nine trips around Earth's equator.

Lunar Landscape

The Moon's rocky surface is marked by craters created millions of years ago by meteorite and asteroid strikes. The largest craters are more than 249 miles (400 km) wide. In 2013, a meteorite 16 inches (40 cm) wide and traveling at 55,923 mph (90,000 km/h) hit the lunar surface. It struck with an impact equal to the explosion of 8,819 pounds (4,000 kg) of dynamite!

DOES THE MOON HAVE GRAVITY?

The Moon only exerts one-sixth of the gravity you find on Earth. While Earth's gravity keeps the Moon in its orbit, the Moon's gravity pulls on Earth too. It causes bulges in the planet's water, which move as Earth rotates to form tides.

MARIA AND MOUNTAINS

Maria are large rocky plains, covered by a layer of rubble and dust 16.4–33 feet (5-10 m) deep. They make up almost one-sixth of the Moon's surface. The Moon also has mountains. The tallest is Mons Huygens, which rises 18,044 feet (5,500 m) above the surrounding area.

Face To Phase

The Moon completes one orbit of Earth in 27.32 Earth days —the same amount of time the Moon takes to complete one spin on its axis. This is known as a synchronous orbit and means that the same side of the Moon always faces Earth. The amount of the Moon lit by the Sun that we can see from Earth is called a phase. To us, the Moon's shape appears to change from a crescent to a full moon over a 29-day cycle.

Astronauts left behind food pouches, used towels, and bags of their urine on the Moon. Yuck!

LUNAR LITTER

Lunar missions have left behind a lot of trash, including broken-down lunar vehicles, crashed space probes, a set of space boots, and a golden olive branch (left there as a sign of peace).

Footprint Fact

The Moon has very little atmosphere and no wind or water to wipe away marks made on its surface. This means that the footprints made by the 12 astronauts who stepped on the Moon during the Apollo missions (1969-1972) are still there.

842 (382)
= THE AMOUNT OF ROCKS IN POUNDS (KG) COLLECTED FROM THE MOON BY ASTRONAUTS DURING THE APOLLO MISSIONS FOR ANALYSIS

MERCURY AND VENUS: STRANGE NEIGHBORS

The two planets nearest to the Sun—Mercury and Venus —are both named after ancient Roman gods. Neither planet has moons, but they are different in many ways.

Mini Mercury

The smallest planet, with a diameter of 3,032 miles (4,879 km), Mercury also has the highest **density**. Battered by meteorite and asteroid strikes, Mercury has dozens of craters, as well as cliffs over 3,280 feet (1,000 m) tall. Since the planet has almost no atmosphere, there are no winds or rain to erode these geographical features. Many are over 3.8 billion years old.

Can you see the smiling face in Mercury's Happy Little Crater?

LONG DAYS, SHORT YEARS

Mercury takes just 88 Earth days to complete its orbit around the Sun. It moves at astounding speed—about 105,633 mph (170,000 km/h). However, the Sun's gravity puts the brakes on Mercury's rotation, making its days very long. The Sun rises on Mercury only once every 176 days!

No planet has a bigger temperature swing than Mercury, which can be as cold as -292°F (-180°C) or as hot as a thermometer-busting 806°F (430°C).

Earth's Twin?

At 7,521 miles (12,104 km) in diameter, Venus is similar in size to Earth and is our nearest neighbor. More than 20 space probes have been sent to explore the planet, but hope of finding more similarities with Earth quickly vanished. Venus has no water on its surface, and its heavy atmosphere presses down with 90 times more force than Earth's atmosphere. One other problem—thick layers of clouds rain down dangerous sulfuric acid.

Sapas Mons

HOW LONG IS A DAY ON VENUS?

As crazy as it sounds, Venus's day (243 Earth days) is longer than its year (224.7 Earth days).

26 (42) MILLION
= THE DISTANCE IN MILES (KM) BETWEEN EARTH AND VENUS, OUR CLOSEST NEIGHBOR

VERY STRANGE VENUS

Venus is a hostile place. Its thick, carbon dioxide-rich atmosphere acts like a blanket, keeping the heat in. The surface of Venus is a sweltering 867°F (464 °C)—hot enough to melt lead! At least 2,000 volcanoes can be found on the planet's surface, including Sapas Mons, a shield volcano 135 miles (217 km) wide—the distance between Austin, Texas and Houston, Texas.

MARS: THE RED PLANET

Mars has fascinated people for thousands of years. The ancient Chinese called it the Fire Star. The ancient Egyptians named it *Her Desher*, which means the Red One.

Meet Mars

Mars is the fourth planet from the Sun, lying an average distance of 142 million miles (227.9 million km) away. The planet is about half the size of Earth, with a diameter of 4,213 miles (6,780 km). It has about 38% of the gravity that Earth has, which means you could jump almost three times higher on Mars.

The length of a day on the red planet is similar to Earth's—24 hours and 37 minutes. But a year on Mars is longer. Mars takes 687 days to complete one orbit around the Sun.

Olympus Mons is the tallest mountain in the entire solar system. It is three times as high as Mount Everest.

WHY IS MARS RED?

Much of Mars is covered by a thick layer of soil containing a large amount of iron-based minerals. The red that you can see is actually rust—iron oxide —formed millions of years ago.

MOONS AND MOUNTAINS

Mars has two tiny moons—Phobos and Deimos— which were first discovered in 1877 by Asaph Hall. These two rocks, which look like giant potatoes, may actually be asteroids captured by Mars's gravity. The largest one, Phobos, is 17 miles (26.8 km) across.

Mars Missions

More than 45 robotic spacecraft have either orbited Mars or landed on its surface. The first successful probe to land was Viking I in 1976. The Curiosity Rover has been moving around the planet gathering information since 2011!

Both NASA (National Aeronautics and Space Administration) and ESA (European Space Agency) plan to send people to Mars by 2040!

The car-sized Curiosity Rover snaps a selfie on Mars after making a 350,000,000 mile (563,000,000 km) journey from Earth.

Life On Mars?

There is no life on Mars today. Some scientists believe that liquid water once ran across the planet's surface. This may have supported some form of life on Mars in the distant past.

TO CAP IT OFF...

Mars has a thin atmosphere made up mostly of carbon dioxide. Temperatures on the planet range from a balmy 77°F (25°C) to a freezing cold -193°F (-125°C) At its two poles, Mars has ice caps made of frozen water and carbon dioxide.

2,485 (4,000)

= THE LENGTH IN MILES (KM) OF THE ENORMOUS VALLES MARINERIS CANYON SYSTEM ON MARS. IF PLACED ON EARTH, THE 124-MILE- (200 KM) WIDE, 4.4-MILE- (7 KM) DEEP CANYON WOULD STRETCH ACROSS THE ENTIRE UNITED STATES.

JUPITER: IT'S MASSIVE!

The biggest planet in the solar system, Jupiter is so large that 1,300 Earth-sized planets could fit inside it. Jupiter has almost two-and-a-half times the mass of all the other planets combined. In other words, it's massive!

Its Place In Space

Jupiter lies an average of 483 million miles (778 million km) from the Sun—about 5.2 times farther from it than Earth. It takes Jupiter 11.86 Earth years to complete an orbit around the Sun, traveling at a speed of just over 29,204 mph (47,000 km/h). From Earth, it's the third-brightest object in the night sky after the Moon and Venus.

NASA's Juno mission is due to reach Jupiter in 2016. It will carry out experiments to help us understand the origin and evolution of the planet.

HOW MANY MOONS DOES JUPITER HAVE?

Jupiter has more moons than any other planet. There are 67 known Jovian moons, four of which (Io, Callisto, Ganymede, and Europa) were first spotted by Italian astronomer, Galileo Galilei, in 1610.

UNDER PRESSURE

Jupiter is known as a gas giant, and its gases, mostly hydrogen and helium, get thicker and denser the closer to the center of the planet you go. At depths of 8,700 miles (14,000 km) or more, massive pressure turns the gases into liquid metal. This gives Jupiter a huge magnetic field that stretches out almost as far as Saturn.

Stunning Stripes

The planet's distinctive stripes are caused by different areas of its atmosphere rising and falling. The lighter, rising bands are called zones. The darker, sinking regions are called belts. The belts contain **molecules** made of hydrogen, oxygen, and carbon. The zones contain clouds of frozen ammonia crystals that reflect sunlight.

zone

belt

The Great Red Spot on Jupiter is big enough to hold two or three Earth-sized planets.

Speedy Spinner

Despite being huge, Jupiter is no slouch. It's the fastest-spinning planet in the solar system, taking only 9 hours, 56 minutes, and 30 seconds to complete a full turn on its axis. This rapid rotation gives the planet a bulge at its equator, as well as flattened north and south poles.

SPOT THE STORM

In 1665, the Italian astronomer Gian Cassini described a feature on Jupiter's surface that we now call the Great Red Spot. It turned out to be an enormous storm, about 1,534 x 746 miles (25,000 x 1,200 km) in size. The storm is still raging today, with 311 mph (500 km/h) winds that make hurricanes on Earth look puny!

88,846 (142,984)

= THE DIAMETER IN MILES (KM) OF JUPITER —ABOUT 11 TIMES LARGER THAN EARTH'S

SATURN: LORD OF THE RINGS

The sixth planet from the Sun, Saturn is the farthest planet that can be seen from Earth without a telescope. It's famous for its stunning rings and many, many moons.

What A Whopper!

With a diameter of 74,898 miles (120,536 km), Saturn is the second-largest planet in the solar system. Despite its giant size, it spins on its axis rapidly. A day on Saturn lasts just 10 hours and 39 minutes, although its year is a lot longer than Earth's. Saturn's journey around the Sun takes more than 29 Earth years to complete.

HOW MANY MOONS DOES SATURN HAVE?

In 1655, Dutch astronomer Christian Huygens was just 26 years old when he used a homemade telescope to become the first person to discover a moon orbiting Saturn. Since his discovery of Titan, 61 more moons have been found.

IT'S A GAS

You couldn't stand on Saturn. Its outer layers are made of gas. The gas is mostly hydrogen, with small amounts of helium and even smaller amounts of other gases, including ammonia and methane. Astronomers think that Saturn might have a rocky, icy core about 7,456 miles (12,000 km) wide—the distance from London, England to Hawaii.

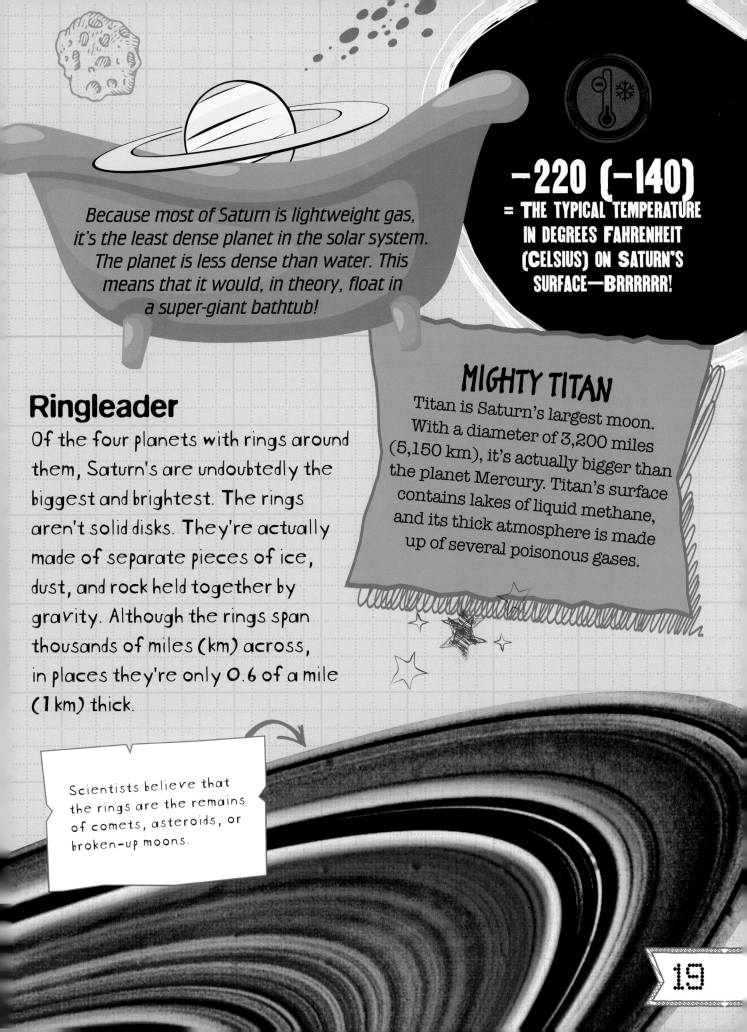

Because most of Saturn is lightweight gas, it's the least dense planet in the solar system. The planet is less dense than water. This means that it would, in theory, float in a super-giant bathtub!

−220 (−140)
= THE TYPICAL TEMPERATURE IN DEGREES FAHRENHEIT (CELSIUS) ON SATURN'S SURFACE—BRRRRRR!

Ringleader

Of the four planets with rings around them, Saturn's are undoubtedly the biggest and brightest. The rings aren't solid disks. They're actually made of separate pieces of ice, dust, and rock held together by gravity. Although the rings span thousands of miles (km) across, in places they're only 0.6 of a mile (1 km) thick.

MIGHTY TITAN

Titan is Saturn's largest moon. With a diameter of 3,200 miles (5,150 km), it's actually bigger than the planet Mercury. Titan's surface contains lakes of liquid methane, and its thick atmosphere is made up of several poisonous gases.

Scientists believe that the rings are the remains of comets, asteroids, or broken-up moons.

URANUS AND NEPTUNE

These two icy giants are far away. Uranus lies an average distance of 1.8 billion miles (2.87 billion km) from the Sun, while Neptune is about 2.8 billion miles (4.5 billion km) away. Both planets receive very little energy from the Sun, so they are seriously cold!

Uranus Or George's Star?

Uranus was discovered in 1781 by the British astronomer William Herschel, who tried to name it after King George III. It was eventually named after the ancient Greek god of the sky. Around 60 Earths would fit inside the 31,763-mile- (51,118 km) diameter planet, which has 11 faint rings around it. A day on Uranus lasts about 17 hours, but a year is much longer since Uranus takes 84 years to orbit the Sun.

WHY IS URANUS ON ITS SIDE?

All the planets are tilted a little on their axes but Uranus's tilt is 98°, meaning the planet orbits the Sun on its side. Many astronomers believe that a really big object once struck the planet causing its dramatic slant.

42

= THE LENGTH IN YEARS OF SUMMER AT URANUS'S NORTH POLE. URANUS'S UNUSUAL SEASONS ARE DUE TO ITS TILT.

Mighty Methane

The eighth and farthest planet from the Sun, Neptune was observed by Galileo as far back as 1612. At 30,778 miles (49,532 km) in diameter, it's slightly smaller than Uranus. It looks blue due to the methane in its atmosphere. Scientists believe that both Neptune and Uranus have small, rocky cores about the size of Earth, which are surrounded by thick layers of gas.

Miranda, the smallest of Neptune's 27 moons, has an unusual, bumpy surface, shown here in this image taken by Voyager 2.

STORMY WEATHER

Voyager 2 is the only spacecraft so far to get up close and personal with Neptune. When it whizzed past in 1989, only 1,864 miles (3,000 km) from the planet's north pole, it showed a huge storm named the Great Dark Spot. The storm is about the size of Earth and has the fastest winds in the solar system at 1,305 mph (2,100 km/h).

Forget celebrating your birthday on Neptune. The planet takes a staggering 164.8 years—over 60,000 days—to complete one orbit of the Sun.

ASTEROIDS AND DWARF PLANETS

The planets are not the only bodies in the solar system to orbit the Sun. Others include dwarf planets and asteroids made up of rock, metal, and ice.

Belt Up

Most asteroids are found in a huge ring called the Main Belt, which lies between the orbits of Mars and Jupiter. Asteroids are believed to be the remains of planets or moons that never fully formed. The Main Belt is mostly empty space because most asteroids are less than 0.6 of a mile (1 km) wide. Only 23 asteroids in the Main Belt are more than 124 miles (200 km) in diameter.

150

= THE NUMBER OF ASTEROIDS DISCOVERED THAT HAVE MINI MOONS ORBITING THEM. SCIENTISTS THINK THERE MAY BE MANY MORE.

ASTEROID ALERT

Some asteroids are quite close to Earth and may cross Earth's orbital path. These are known as Near Earth Asteroids (NEAs) and are tracked by space agencies in case any appear to be dangerously close. In 2014, a 214-foot- (370 m) long NEA called 2014 HQ124 passed close to Earth—about 3.25 times the distance between Earth and the Moon.

A massive asteroid impact in Yucatán, Mexico, 65 million years ago, is believed to have caused the extinction of dinosaurs.

Poor Old Pluto

Discovered by Clyde Tombaugh in 1930, Pluto reigned supreme for 76 years as the smallest planet in the solar system. But in 2006, it received a downgrade, becoming a dwarf planet. Pluto is extremely distant—between 2.7 billion and 5.6 billion miles (4.4 billion and 7.4 billion km) away from the Sun. It takes 248 years to complete its orbit.

Pluto is depicted here with its largest moon, Charon, and two of its smaller **satellites**.

DWARF PLANETS

Dwarf planets aren't moons because they orbit the Sun, not a planet. They are big enough for gravity to have pulled them into round shapes, but not big enough for gravity to clear their orbital path of rocks or ice. The dwarf planet Ceres is found in the asteroid belt, while Eris and Pluto lie on the outskirts of the solar system, beyond Neptune.

WHO NAMED PLUTO?

An 11-year-old schoolgirl, Venetia Burney, suggested naming Pluto after the Roman god of the underworld. Her grandfather passed the idea on to his astronomer friends, and it was accepted!

Earth's Moon
2,160 miles (3,476 km) in diameter

Eris
1,445 miles (2,326 km)

Ceres
590 miles (950 km)

Earth
7,918 miles (12,742 km)

This illustration shows the size of dwarf planets compared to Earth and our Moon.

Charon
728 miles (1,172 km)

Pluto
1,471 miles (2,368 km)

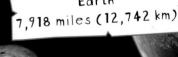

23

METEORS AND METEORITES

Earth is under attack from space! Around 110 tons (100 metric tons) of material hurtles toward our planet every day. Among this space debris are meteoroids, which usually burn up in Earth's atmosphere or fall to the ground as meteorites.

Rock 'n' Metal

Meteoroids are pieces of rock or metal that travel through space, pulled toward Earth by our planet's gravity. Many are fragments of asteroids but some are debris from comets, the Moon, or Mars.

Over 100 meteors can be seen every hour in the Geminids meteor shower, which happens each year in mid-December.

TAKE A SHOWER

Most meteoroids burn up in the atmosphere in seconds. These are called meteors. Some meteors melt and form streaks of light in the night sky, known as shooting stars. A collection of meteors appearing within a short time span is known as a meteor shower.

HOW FAST DO METEORS TRAVEL?

The fastest meteors enter Earth's atmosphere at a speed of 161,059 mph (259,200 km/h).

Impact!

Meteoroids that make it to Earth are called meteorites. Some larger meteorites create craters on impact. One in Arizona, called simply Meteor Crater, was formed around 50,000 years ago. A 164 foot (50 m) meteorite crashed into the ground at a speed of more than 27,961 mph (45,000 km/h) creating this impact crater, which is 557 feet (170 m) deep and 75 miles (1.2 km) wide.

Meteor Crater

132,277 (60,000)
= THE WEIGHT IN POUNDS (KG) OF THE HEAVIEST METEORITE EVER FOUND ON EARTH, KNOWN AS THE HOBA METEORITE

Bruising Encounter

Ann Elizabeth Hodges is the only person ever proven to have been struck by a meteorite. A 9 pound (4.4 kg) rock from space crashed through her roof in Alabama in 1954 and bruised her left hand and hip.

COMETS

Comets are chunks of rock, dust, and ice that travel through space like large, dirty snowballs. They can be anywhere from a few hundred yards or meters to 25 miles (40 km) in size. Comets come from beyond the planets in our solar system.

Burning Up

All comets orbit the Sun, but most of them remain so far from Earth that we cannot see them. However, the orbit of some comets brings them in toward the inner planets. There, energy from the Sun heats the comet up turning its ice to gas. This forms a hazy head, or coma, around the nucleus of the comet.

A LONG TAIL

Tails also form behind a comet. One tail contains dust and one contains gas. These can trail a long way behind the nucleus. The tail of Comet Hyakutake has been measured at 354 million miles (570 million km) long—that's almost the distance between Earth and Jupiter!

gas tail

dust tail

coma

Comet Hale-Bopp was visible to the naked eye from Earth between 1996 and 1997.

Comet Hyakutake was discovered in 1996 by an amateur astronomer in Japan using only a pair of binoculars!

Hairy Stars

Comets have been observed in the night sky for centuries. The word comet is Greek for "hairy star." The most famous comet of all is Halley's Comet, named after Edmond Halley, who calculated that it would reappear in the night sky every 76 years.

Halley's Comet appears in the Bayeux Tapestry, a depiction of a famous battle, created in the 11th century.

COMET HUNTER

American Carolyn Shoemaker only took up astronomy when she was 51. She made up for lost time, however. She discovered 32 comets and more than 300 asteroids! One of the comets she co-discovered, Shoemaker-Levy 9, crashed into Jupiter in 1994 at a speed of over 124, 274 mph (200,000 km/h).

250,000

= THE ESTIMATED LENGTH IN YEARS OF COMET WEST'S ORBIT. DON'T WAIT UP!

Comet West was strikingly visible from Earth in 1976.

HOW LONG DOES A COMET'S ORBIT LAST?

Some comets have short orbits lasting less than 20 years, which means they become a regular, repeating feature in the night sky. Long-period comets take more than 200 years to complete an orbit, so if you've seen them once, you won't see them again!

EXOPLANETS

The solar system is not the only place in the universe where planets are found. Astronomers have always suspected that there might be planets orbiting stars other than the Sun, but they didn't have proof until the 1990s.

Needle In A Haystack

Trying to find **exoplanets** in the vastness of space is hard. The planets are huge distances away from Earth and are usually outshone by the stars they orbit. Planet hunters use a range of techniques to find exoplanets, including trying to spot the slight dimming of light from a star when an exoplanet travels in front of it.

ULTIMATE EXOPLANET FINDER

The Kepler Telescope is the ultimate exoplanet hunter. Between its launch in 2009 and the middle of 2014, it helped discover a staggering 977 exoplanets. These include Kepler-16b, the first known exoplanet to orbit not one but two stars, and Kepler-70b, a planet that whizzes around its star in less than six hours!

Like something out of a sci-fi film, two suns set over the horizon of Kepler-16b.

Peculiar Planets

There are some strange exoplanets out there, including GJ 504b, which is a young, bright-pink planet, and HD 209458b, which takes just 3.3 days to orbit its star. Winds of over 3,107 mph (5,000 km/h) race through the atmosphere of HD 189733b , an exoplanet that contains high levels of silica, the material from which glass is made. Some scientists have suggested that the planet may experience glass raining down on its surface.

WILL WE EVER FIND ANOTHER EARTH?

One day, astronomers hope to find a rocky world with a thick, oxygen-rich atmosphere and surface water. Sound familiar? The search mainly focuses on something called a habitable zone, where an exoplanet orbits its star at the right distance to provide enough heat to support life without being too hot.

Glass And Diamonds

If you think glass raining down is bizarre, check out exoplanet 55 Cancri e. About one third of this exoplanet is composed of carbon. One theory scientists have is that the carbon may all be in diamond form because of the enormous pressure it experiences!

3,992 (2,200)
= THE SURFACE TEMPERATURE IN DEGREES FAHRENHEIT (CELSIUS) OF EXOPLANET WASP-12B —HOT ENOUGH TO MELT STEEL!

GLOSSARY

atmosphere The gases surrounding the surface of a planet

axis An imaginary line that goes through the center of an object that is spinning

bodies Objects in space

density A measure of how much matter an object contains in its volume. If something is very dense, then it contains a lot of matter in a small space.

diameter The distance across the middle of a circle or through the middle of a sphere

equator The imaginary line around the middle of Earth

exoplanet Planets orbiting stars other than Earth's Sun

mass The amount of matter an object contains

matter Physical things that exist in space, such as solids, liquids, or gases

molecule The smallest unit of a substance that is composed of two or more atoms

molten Rock or metal turned into liquid due to heat

nucleus/nuclei (pl.) The center of an object or an atom

orbit To travel around another object in space, usually in an elliptical path

radiation Different kinds of energy from heat or light

satellite An object that moves around another object in space

spacecraft Vehicles that either orbit in space or land on a certain location in space

spherical Something that has the shape of a sphere (a 3-D circle)

FURTHER INFORMATION

Books

20 Fun Facts about Asteroids and Comets
by Arielle Chiger (Gareth Stevens, 2014)

Our Solar System
by Seymour Simon (Harper Collins, 2014)

The Planets 2014
by Robert Dinwiddie, Heather Couper, John Farndon,
Nigel Henbest, David Hughes, Giles Sparrow
(DK, 2014)

Websites

https://solarsystem.nasa.gov/planets
The latest news and amazing images of space
from NASA

http://science.nationalgeographic.com/science/
space/solar-system
An excellent guide to the solar system

www.bbc.co.uk/science/space/solarsystem
Information and videos about our solar system
and its planets.

INDEX